Words that Burn

Wayne F. Burke

BareBackPress

This is a work of fiction. The characters, incidents, and dialogue are the products of the author's imagination and are not to be construed as real. Any resemblance to actual events or person, living or dead, is entirely coincidental.

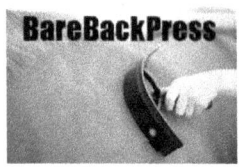

BareBackPress
Hamilton, Ontario, Canada
For enquires visit www.barebackpress.com
For information contact press@barebacklit.com

Cover design and layout © Choi Yunnam

No part of this book may be used or reproduced in any manner whatsoever without written permission, except in the case of brief quotations embodied in critical articles and reviews. For information address BareBackPress.

Portions of this book have previously appeared in other publications: '86'd,' 'In the Chelsea Jail,' 'Arise & Shine,' 'Harvard,' 'Barefoot,' 'Half-A-Cop,"From the Columbia Point Housing Project, Southie,'(Boston Poetry Magazine), 'A Shit,' 'Never Had a Room,' 'Slut,' 'Piss Test,' (Bareback), 'The Long Walk,' (Visions With Voices), 'Red,' 'Courtyard,' (The Commonline Journal), 'Snapshot, 1957,' 'Rat,' (Sassafras), 'Cooked,' (Industry Night), 'Ascension,' (as 'Slave Revolt') (miller's pond).

COPYRIGHT © 2013 Wayne F. Burke
All RIGHTS RESERVED
ISBN-10: 0992035511
ISBN-13: 978-0992035518

Words that Burn
Wayne F. Burke

POEMS

I
Last Kiss
Vests
TV Land
Rookie
Never Had A Room
The Cane
Snapshot, 1957
Piss Test
Big Kids
II
Hot summer
Late Bloomer
Man
A Chick
Young Love
Lust
A Shit
A Cute Young Thing
Relations
Slut
A Hole In One
Neiman Marcus Jeans
III
What I Am

Arise & Shine
Hurry hurry
Stickers
Loneliness
IV
ID'd
86'd
Red
The Chelsea jail
Harvard
Resting
I Move to Vermont
V
From Columbia Point Housing Project, Southie
Poetry Reading
Big Al
Life Is Funny
Pseudo-Artists and Gigolos
Teacher
VI
Ascension
Where Were You?
Rat
Words
Cooked
Barefoot
Prisoners

Half-A-Cop
VII
Struggle
No Therapist
By-Pass
The Park
Spring
The Long Walk
Heartburn
Courtyard
Attempted Murder, 3rd Degree
Heat
Punks
VIII
The Irish Sea
Sunday
IX
The Days of Our Lives
The Drunkards
As the Worm Turns

Forward

I am not in favor of "forwards." I do not usually read them. I am writing this "forward" only because my publisher (whom I suspect of sadism and other un-pleasantries) requested I do so. What is there to say, after all, about one's own book of poems? One can say that one wrote them. One can say that one had fun writing some, less fun writing others. Why did one write them, you ask? One replies that one has no fucking clue. One further replies: why not? Why does the bird sing? one asks. Why does the cow moo? Why does one ask such goofy questions? Again: no clue. One is clueless. One leaves all analysis of such things to ones better qualified. One ain't no critic. One secretly suspects that one wrote these poems, and others, because one is a bigger jackass than one's publisher (the dirty old...). One often contradicts oneself (doesn't one?). One often thinks one's poems to be worthless; one often thinks one's poems to be the greatest thing since sliced bread. One can, however, be wrong about such things; one can also be right. What one thinks about one's work however, does not matter (not to one who reads the work) one like you, dear reader. Or one other.

Wayne F. Burke

To my parents:
Edward (1926-1958)
Claire (1928-1956)

I

The sun's bright eye
is zeroed in

the zeros add up
and multiply

as the sunflower bends

as we lose and win
but mostly lose
and seek an hour in the sun
zeroed in
idle and unburdened
lolling
through numbered days
hours
moving toward an end

Last Kiss

Moving from mouth to mouth
kissing every girl in the bar
their boyfriends stand aside and
stare and one bitch has a fit after
I smack her lips and soon I am
outside and lying on the sidewalk
beneath a tree and listening to
wind rustle through the leaves
and if god has a voice that is it
the soothing shush and rush of
sibilance, the whispered hush and
sudden gust of exhaled breath
calming me but not enough
because later I climbed the side of
a building and broke in through
a third floor window and came to
sitting on a bed in a dark room
and heard the footsteps of a giant
outside the door which flew open
to let a cop in who handcuffed me
so tightly the cuffs stayed on my wrists
for years.

Vests

A yellow jacket on a dandelion
does not have a jacket on but a
fuzzy sort of vest, like mohair
sweaters girls in my high school wore
that made their tits—those who had
them—resemble snow cones. High
School was a prison with a vice-principal
patrolling the yard. Bells told us when to
move. Most kids were going nowhere
except to work. I had ambition and
sweat rings beneath my arm pits and
pimples on my face. I got drunk on
Saturday nights and chased cock-teasers.
Beat up hippies. Wore a red football jacket
with white lightning bolts down the sleeves;
name and number across the chest. Only
queers and nerds wore vests.

TV Land

Sitting in front of the black & white
television
watching Danny Thomas,
Andy of Mayberry, Darren & Samantha...
All their problems were solved in half an hour,
while mine were never solved at all.
The Beaver, Chip, Ernie, Opie, Little Ricky...
They had it made. Nobody ever beat the shit
out of them. No big kids tortured them. They
never peed the bed. They did not eat SPAM.
They did not take baths in the sink. They did
not have nocturnal emissions. They did not
get worms. They were not beat with hair brush
or belt. They were not told to go outside and
to stay there...They had it good. In TV Land.

Rookie

Clam Diggers, Ring Dings, Good & Plenty,
Tar Babies, Rob & Laura Petrie...
I trained my arm to make the long
throw from third to first.
I was another Brooks Robinson
or at least Frank Malzone,
though I did not take many ground balls
off my chest because I did not have
much of a chest or much of anything...
Had a glove handed down from my
brother. Had a bed to sleep in. Had a
name and so-called family. What else?
Had a snowball's chance in hell but
did not know that then. Did not know
much. Knew I wanted to play. Knew I
was better than most. Knew a few of
the state capitals, and names of some
dinosaurs. Knew I was alone:
or at least suspected as much.

Never had A Room

Never had a room of my own until
I was sixteen,
always had a bed;
my two brothers and uncle
had beds too
in the same room;
my uncle came home late
stomping up stairs and
falling into bed like a tree trunk
into empty cans;
his snores were like a language
of the deaf and dumb;
in the morning he retched
into the toilet then stumped
to his bed—fat man on Popsicle stick legs—
and sat to put on his gas station uniform
grunting as he bent
to tug up socks.
A bastard he could be
who gave me backhanded slaps
and kicks from size ten shoes and
once whipped me with his belt
as I squirmed on the back yard lawn

howling loud enough for the neighbors and
the world to hear
but they never did.

The Cane

Dark clouds slide in:
dark as the closet
I was shoved into
after I hid Grandma's
cane—
the mahogany one she hit us with.

She looked for it high and low
up, down, and in between.
Finally, she asked me
"where is it? You hid it—
didn't you?"

I only knew my name, rank, and
serial number.

My brother wanted to tell.
I held him to the floor
but he broke free when my uncle
came home from work at noon.

My uncle bounced me like a basketball
across the hallway floor
and threw me into the closet

and shut and locked the door.

I sat with moth balls
flying over rubber feet;
Gramp's silk ties hung
on a rack.
I beat on the door until Uncle returned
and I heard the key turn
and leapt
between his legs after
the door opened
and ran
off the front porch steps
and onto the grass
and down the street
as he shouted
"come back here!"
in a voice
that died in air.

Snapshot, 1957

The sound of the rain—its patter and drip
is as soothing as being held in my father's grip
above his head as he lies face-up on the ground,
my mother sitting at a picnic table in the background.
My father has a white t-shirt on and is looking at me
while I soar at the ends of his arms, a turkey-shaped bundle,
in the air, looking ahead.

Piss Test

I had stomach aches.
They finally took me to see
a specialist in the big city.
A nurse brought me into a bathroom
and said "stand there," and pointed
to a spot by the door.
I stood and watched her place a cup
on top of the toilet across the room.
"Do you see that cup?" she asked. "Pee in it,"
and she left.
I looked at the cup. It was far away.
I took my bibet out and aimed.
I got some in but mostly missed.
The nurse returned: she said "what have you done?"
and began to yank paper towels from the dispenser
like she was pulling out someone's hair.

The specialist told me to lie on a table.
He looked at my fesse and I laughed and
my Grandfather, who brought me, laughed too
and the doctor's face turned fire engine red.

I had worms.

Big Kids

The big kids held us down
and tapped with their fingertips
on our chests until we laughed
then cried then laughed and cried
then laughed and cried and screamed
then laughed and cried and screamed
and begged for mercy.
I was known as the kid who could take it:
take more punishment than the others.
The big kids admired me for being able to take it.
And it seemed like I was always taking it:
slaps, the belt, the hairbrush, torture, tappers
kicks in the ass…taking it and taking it
until I got big enough to give it too.

II

with the mouse and the sparrow

with the bums and the misshapen

on the railroad tracks and
under the bridges
in the bar rooms and
the institutions.

at the edge of the circle

on the streets of
rinky-dink towns that
no one visits unless they
too
are lost.

Hot Summer

After an hour or two
of making out with
her
I would have a hard-on
like a bar of soap
but she would never
touch it
or even acknowledge
that I had more in
my pocket
than loose change and
when her mother coughed
twice from the living room
it was time for her
to go into the house
and me to walk home
beneath the moon
with my piece
of rebar
that I never used
for anything that summer
except piss out of.

Late Bloomer

I did not jerk off until
I was fifteen and then
it was by accident.
Did not get laid until
I was eighteen
and even then it was
not my doing but
the girl's, who had
pulled my cock out
and sat on top
and I slid in
half-hard
feeling pleasure
and when she jumped off
I shot
and the wind roared
and the car rocked
and my cousin and his girl
stood in the window
their faces dark smudges
against the steamed-up glass
and I heard the girl ask:
"what are they doing in there?"

Man

I met her in the dorm and
according to my buddy
she went outside after I left
and said to her girlfriend:
"I met a man!"
The next night I fucked her
and then booked, leaving her on the bed
forever.
My buddy told me
"that girl is someone's sister;
would you want someone to treat
your sister like you treated that girl?"
I had not thought of it that way.
I did not think of things like that:
I thought mostly about myself.
I was not a man.

A Chick

She knocked and walked into my room
wearing a towel that covered only half
her ass.
"Got a match?" she asked.
I looked in the drawer and in the desk.
"No," I said, "sorry."
She gave me a funny look as she left
and she never came back.

Young Love

She was anxious to fuck.
No talking, hurry up
get in position
and buck.
We had two kids together,
both went out with the garbage.
After the second she had postpartum —
a depressed girl, would not get out of bed
ate chocolates and wept,
ground her teeth as she slept.
One night she punched me
because, she said
I killed her kids.
But I did not do it.
We both did.

Lust

A girl with bullet-shaped
tits
I once lusted after
for a year —
I saw her on the street
yesterday
and could not remember her name —
just the tits.

A Shit

I just took a shit.
It felt good coming out
and now, I see
the sun has come out
also
and maybe spring
is on the way
through I would not bet much
on its arrival
any time soon
and my guess is that
she
who used to visit me
is not coming again —
she, who used my toilet
and complained to me
about her boyfriend,
she, who would not have sex
because, she said, she
is celibate…
Celibate my ass
or rather
her ass

which, I have noticed
has become bigger
lately
and flabbier
and jiggles
as she moves,
clueless,
to
nobody knows where.

A Cute Little Thing

She was a cute little thing
with big doe eyes
and bright smile
and as we kissed one night in front
of the dormitory
after our first date
she squeezed my cock
in her little gloved hand
and the next night
I was sleeping in her room;
she in a bathrobe and chirping
like a bird at dawn
and me high on pot
and without a condom on.
Whenever we sat outside I put my
head in her lap and
she stroked my hair;
it was something nice
bright like her smile
but
when the semester ended
she came to me crying
and hysterical

but would not say why

and I went away

but

remained inside her.

Relations

She was older than me
and had a gimpy leg
and
the first time we went to bed
I could not get it up.
Hell, I thought
should I go back to drinking?
The next time was better
but not much
as I had to over use
imagination to enjoy
the fuck.
I dumped her and became
involved with a blonde
with big tits,
one tit bigger than the other.
She was a "born again" and
ditzy; wanted me to tell her
how to run her life, which
I could not, would not, do.
She went back to her ex-
husband, a porno addict,
and I went back to doing.

Slut

She is an ex-cheerleading
slut
who fucked every guy
in the apartment
except me.
I don't know why not
me:
I was willing enough,
but did not play the game
right, I guess;
did not even know a game was being played.
In high school I was the guy
who gave the girl a ride home
after the gang-bang;
the guy who protected the
drunk girl;
the guy who gave the naked girl
a shirt;
the guy who tried to save girls' virtue…
The fool.

A Hole in One

She pulled on my dink as
we sat in the car, the radio
on, the golf course dark;
I watched her white hand stroke.
"My arm is getting tired," she said
and the hand stopped.
I felt like punching her
and ripping off her dress.
"Just a little longer," I begged.
She sighed and the hand moved
up and down and
I shot a wad onto the dash
and onto her hand
which she held up to the moon light
and asked "what do I do with it?"
meaning my cum
and I said "lick it off," or should have said
but did not;
instead, I found a Kleenex
and gave it
to
the dumb cluck.

Neiman Marcus Jeans

As the train clattered into the station
I put my hand between the
woman's legs and felt the
soft material of her jeans and
lumpiness of her cunt.
"HOW DARE YOU,' she said
like an actress in a lousy play.
Two shopping bags hung
from her shoulders —
one read NEIMAN MARCUS.
Her eyes smoldered.
The pneumatic doors opened
and I got off.

III

throw a dog to the bone

the night bleeds ink

I scratch these words
in stone

What I Am

A stone, a leaf, a scrap
of paper in the street I
walk down running a
gauntlet of cars going
elsewhere everywhere
the sky weighs me down
this morning and the sun
says fuck you as the bums
in the park measure me
with their eyes staring
their staring eyes my
first cup of coffee goes
down like a rock I am
a rock, a stone, a leaf
a candy wrapper on the
street I walk down my
feet in cement glued to
past event the memory
in my head will climb
to the third story the
cat burglar who enters
and steals the past let
it go for christ sakes

it has gone water over
the barn, the coop has
flown, a leaf, a twig,
a stone, me, the street
a bridge of clouds I
climb to the precipice
and let go my feet in
the dust and ashes of
this old street dead end
road, rock, stone, leaf,
orange peel, wrapper.

Arise & Shine

A slow poke to China in a sore
morning
I shouldered-on all night
soldier-boying
on the good ship Lollipop
going nowhere
rolling
in the Irish stew
of myself
thinking if only
but knowing it could not be other
wise
and finally sleeping
feeling forsaken
and waking to nothing
more or
less and
getting on with it
the business of so-called living
bare feet on kitchen floor
the linoleum of life
carpet of the poor
padding through to the living room

and looking out at clouds

and taking the rope off

I had put on like a turtleneck

and flying

out the door

like a buttercup

through a meadow of daisies.

Hurry Hurry

The pleasure of
being alone and
reading a book
while the world
goes on with its madness
its mad people going
as fast as
they can
over and through
others
in the mad scramble
to get somewhere:
the next appointment
the next street light
the next corner
the next fix:
the accomplishment of
getting there fast
faster:
getting there and
then
getting to the next
goal

to the next

game

to the next

whatever:

the next the next the next

to the grave.

Stickers

They have these stickers,
ribbons, on their cars
to show support for the troops:
One ribbon: moron.
Two ribbons: congenital moron.
The government supports troops
and I support the government by
paying taxes
and if the government fails
then vote the bastards out
get some new bastards in
it is called politics
a shitty game,
like the writing business
full of loathsome shits,
like every business
like prostitution
what is your price?
Fifty bucks for a beaver shot?
Hundred and a half for your soul?
A cold wind blows
everywhere
not just in the north:

the dark hole of Mexico
in everyone's backyard:
it is called the system
and it sucks.

Loneliness

My Grandmother
did not like
being alone:
she had
television
and
housework
and monthly visits
from her son
and
from her daughter
and the newspaper
and prayer
but no longer any one
to do for,
and she had been doing for
all her life.
That is why she put up
with me
who did not work
or pay rent
who came home drunk
and passed-out on the floor:

she had someone to do for

and did

even when I did not want it

done.

IV

grow the seed

spread the leaf

cover the spread

fit the cover

tighten the fit

right the snugness

assure the rightness

give the assurance

beget the given

riven the misbegotten

weld the rivet

hold the meld

ID'd

I came to
in the dark
of my room
I was covered in mud
And could not undo the laces of my shoes
so lit a match
and set them on fire.

Where had I been?
What had I done?

The cops came two days later
in shiny cruisers
on a sunny afternoon in the city,
from different directions
to cut me off in the middle
of a crosswalk.

It had been a good day up until then.

One of the cops threw me
onto the hood of the car
and another cop handcuffed
me.

Me, the "unidentified man"
of a newspaper story
in the morning edition.

The cops knew who I was
but I did not.

The bartender knew
I did not need
another drink, but I knew
I did, and so
after being shut-off
I had climbed over the bar
and made my own
and when the bartender cuffed the glass
from my hand
I had punched him,
according to the police report,
then had run out of the bar
and had become "unidentified"
until the cops showed
in the middle of the road.

86'd

After working a ten-hour shift in the restaurant
I went to a bar
in Central Square
that served beer in 16 ounce milkshake glasses
and I was on my fourth or fifth
when this broad
with stringy hair, not
washed in a coon's age,
wearing a leather vest—
some type of biker chick—
poked me in the ribs and
said "hey Bub, you're in
my seat," and I said "hey
Sister, go bother someone
else," and she got hold of
my hair and yanked
my head down to the floor
and when she let go
I slapped her across the face
and she went out
on her feet
her eyes two stars—
Raggedy Anne falling back

against the guy next to me —
and someone said "how dare you"
and someone else sucker-punched
me and I was on the floor
and it was dark
and someone kicked me in the face
and someone kicked me in the ribs
and luckily I had sat near the door
and made my way through kick after kick
and out into the quiet street
as people from the bar chased me
up the bricks.

Red

The drunker I got
the more I fought
to stay sober, and
the straighter I
stood, until, ready
to pass out, I strode
from the bar to the
nearest car in the lot
and into the backseat
took a header...
One night I woke as the
car I'd slept in moved at
a high rate of speed down
a hill and a guy I knew, "Red,'
driving, ramming the nose
of his car into the rear of a
car ahead. "What the fuck
are you doing?" I said to Red
who, surprised to see me, said
his girlfriend was with a guy in
the other car and that he, Red,
was
going to kill both.

I had to talk fast that night:
had to save 3 lives, 4, including
my own; had to get Red to agree
to wait and kill the bastards later.

The Chelsea Jail

The night of the Ali-Ernie Shavers fight
I was at My Brother's Place
a bar near the Greyhound bus station downtown
and drinking gin & tonics
which were going down smooth
and I decided, after the fight, to take
a bus to Chelsea and
drink in a bar called "Heaven's Gate."
And I was having a good time
feeling-up girls
until a fat guy said
that I had to leave
and I said "why?"
and he said "you are pinching the broads' asses
and they do not like it,"
and he and his buddies
hustled me out
into the pouring rain
and cold dark street
and I stood,
excluded from life's party,
and brooded until
I decided to go back in

but a half-a-cop at the door
said "you can't come in,"
and I balled my fist
and marked a spot on his
cheekbone where light
from a streetlamp glimmered
and I started to swing
but a voice
from Planet Crouton spoke
"no"
and I walked up the sidewalk
to the corner and a box
in the gutter
with a rock inside
a dinosaur egg
waiting to be discovered
and I turned and flung the stone —
a Don Drysdale heater —
through the bar room window
then ran
up the rain-slick street
until my shoe came off
and I stopped to pick it up
as two guys from the bar
wearing softball uniforms

caught hold of me.

One guy held my arms

the other guy wailed punches —

Ernie Shavers haymakers —

against my head

until the paddy wagon

pulled to the curb and

the two guys and half-a-cop

threw me inside

and I was driven to the Police Station

and booked

and listened to a guy in the next cell

sing 'Lord I Want to Go Home'

all night long

while people from the bar

waited outside the jail for me

to be bailed out —

which

did not happen.

Harvard

It was November
and cold
and I drank a pint
of Jack Daniels
then slept on a bench
in the park
and when I woke
had an indent in the back
of my head from the bench.
I had no place
but had a job
as janitor
at Harvard University
where I cleaned the insides of buildings
and drank whatever whiskey
I found in the professors' desks;
I slept on their couches too
and one morning got caught sleeping
by the supervisor,
a Cuban woman, who was more concerned
with being attractive than in being
boss
and she gave me a break

by not firing me

and gave me another break

later on

but

when I got caught making a telephone call

long distance

from the Dean of Admissions office

she said that

she had to let me go.

Resting

Sleeping on a nice comfortable
bed of grass
beside the sidewalk
outside the hotel,
cars passing
people walking by,
I am awakened by a cop
who looks like Marshall Dillon.
"You can't sleep here," he says
like a vice-principal to a fuck-up.
I haul myself up like a load of brick
and stumble, on broken feet
to the park across the street and lie
in a new bed
one far less comfortable.

I Move to Vermont

I am standing in a crowded bar room
talking to a girl
and the girl slaps me across the face
(for why, I don't know)
and then some guy
runs into me
and I go back about fifteen feet and
hit the floor and
curl into the fetal position
to protect my private parts and head
and I wait
and wait
but no one tries to kick me in the nuts
or stomp on my face
and I stand
and think
"what a great place"
and I have been here since:
twenty-five years.

v

the shadows lengthen

the comet approaches

the coming apocalypse does not arrive

the needle enters

the poets lie

the gods call-in sick

the boss demands more hours of your life

the dump truck snores in the yard

the beautiful people shit in the toilet

the sky unfolds its lovely wings

and the bird soars

From Columbia Point Housing Project, Southie

He was the one who told me

write about what you know about

and that a bad childhood

was relevant.

He was the one

inspired—

moving toward destiny.

The one who asked

Don't you love me anymore?

and

How often do we get together, anyway?

He caught everyone

On the rebound

or

On the flip-flop.

He said to girls

Chivalry is not dead.

He called tough guys

Pumpkin.

He read people

like books;

Told them they were Looking Good

in their old age,

Looking Spiffy.

He called them Ace

and Big Time.

He said

It is not a conspiracy

he said

Talk about what you know about

he said

No one ever said it was going to be easy

he said

Let's blow this pop stand

he said

I need a drink.

He called all dogs

Poochie.

He was on fire

alight with his genius:

Robert E. Clifford.

Poetry Reading

The auditorium of the Boston Public Library
is sparsely filled
forty or fifty people, not more.
Jimmy Steinman hands me a beer,
good old Steinman
knows his ass from his elbow —
we drink to Richard Hugo's health,
the poet appears,
looking embarrassed
bald, overweight
he eyeballs Steinman and me
as we drink,
Jimmy slumps in his seat.
We are poets too, like Hugo
I think,
and so does Jimmy
though he refuses to meet
Richard
afterward.

Big Al

He showed up at State College
as guest lecturer,
his face brick red and
a briefcase he kept his
poems and booze in;
wore a corduroy jacket
that looked as if bought
on his way from the shop.
Battered dickie slacks
and hush puppy shoes;
you could smell his B.O. from
across the room; he was poet laureate
and he smoked hash at the party,
given in his honor,
from a pipe passed between me, Stoner,
and Birddog in a kitchen corner.
He told me believe everything
Lowry wrote about Mexico and
nothing Lawrence wrote about the country;
said he liked Kerouac when Jack was
"right in there"; admired Corso as a
character; liked Bukowski, "the bar room guy."
His wife was a daughter of

a famous artist:

she called him "Dugan":

my buddy and me called him "Big Al"

and liked him because he was

not only book smart

but street wise.

Life Is Funny

David Brown died. He said he
would never forgive me and
I wonder if he ever did. I set up
a poetry reading for me, him, and
two others: David read first and
so nervously he shook and warbled
words in a tremulous quaver as
the audience felt sorry for him.
He blamed me. The poems were
not bad either; he had an aura of
solitude and was so unprepossessing
that he stood out in a crowd. A wispy
Quaker beard made him look older
but he was bright eyed and stung by
eternal youth...And now he is dead and
I am alive. Have I been elected to survive
and he to die? Who knows...Life is strange.

Pseudo-Artists and Gigolos

I lived with Steinman and Arturo
in a house in Somerville, outside
Boston. Steinman was a poet and
Arturo an artist, but neither made
much poetry or art, but did make
plenty of girls — girls with names
like 'Bubbles' and 'Sunshine' and
'Merrie' — in and out the door.
I slept on a mattress on the floor
and did not make any girls because
the girls were not interested in me:
I got drunk and high and woke in the
morning by myself and hung over
and pulled my unwashed janitor's
uniform on and caught the number 10
bus into the city, stuffed like a toe in
a sock; another foot in the race, sweating
and feeling bad, ready to puke as I pushed
a vacuum cleaner, set up chairs, trashed...
I climbed stairs to the roof of the hotel to
read or sleep. I was the only white guy until
Frank got hired: I liked the black guys better.
Frank had dead eyes, a broad plane of a face

and he hated "niggers." One of the blacks, Cooney, hated "honkies," especially me. He was happy as shit on the day he said the boss wanted to see me...I knew what was coming, so did Cooney. Being fired was no big deal: hell, I was an artist not a janitor.

Teacher

My college buddy and fellow artist
painted and sculpted and
spoke of Cezanne and Picasso
and Henry Moore
and of what they accomplished
and how.
Then he became a teacher of art
in a high school
and he is still at it, thirty years
only he no longer paints or sculpts
and will not talk about art at all
and instead of silk he wears lead
and instead of a cap a helmet
and instead of a smile a scowl
and instead of a car he drives a tank
and instead of a human being he acts
just like any other
bourgeois
motherfucker.

VI

as the faucet drips

as the lies accumulate

as the dirty looks multiply

as the cup drinks itself dry

as the skunk mates with the owl

as the sun circles the earth

as the mouse chases the hawk

as the wrist cuts the razor

as the landlord pays the rent

as the mailman bites the dog

as the water burns the fire

as the porcupine writes a letter

with its quill and sends it to

the cat, who has befriended the rat

as ocean falls into sea

Ascension

Gramp, more Claudian than Augustan
died
and unlike Christ
failed to rise on the 3rd day
or any other…
Uncle Albert,
brazen as any Nero,
at the head of the table
sat
wrapped in layers of fat
thick as walls keeping Chinas' in or out:
I ran like a coolie to uncle's shouts.
Agrippina-Gram limped from stove to
sink to table serving meat and potato.
My sister gnawed a bone; my brother
impersonated a clam…Uncle, the Great-
Man-of-the-Dinner-Table, ruled with
an iron hand, only his rules changed
like his moods, from black to blacker,
and I was always wrong, crooked somehow
in need of being straightened by a kick
from size ten shoes, or a slap of his calloused
hand—

Gram folded her wooden lap: she bled the years
together and was caught in the groove of a record
going round —
I failed to wipe several different looks off my face.
I had insurrection in mind.
I was Spartacus against the power of Rome
and I lost every time.

Where Were You?

Miss Good, a talcum-powdered bag of flesh
rapped our knuckles bloody with a ruler
stuck her beauty parlor hairdo
through the door
of the grade 4 classroom
called to Mrs. LaBoy "come here."
Mrs. LaBoy stood in front of the class
hands clasped behind her back
her short unwashed flapper-style hairdo
plastered to her skull like a shower cap;
we called her Olive Oyl behind her back.
She slapped me whenever I got out of line
and on Parents-Teacher night told my
grandparents I was reform school bound.
I hated her guts as much as she hated mine
and I made a pain of myself in her skinny bum.
It was 1963; people were still dumb as bricks;
Mrs. LaBoy cleared her Popsicle stick throat:
"The President," she said, "has been shot."

Rat

Gramp took me to the back room
of his bar where beer kegs and empties
were stored, and a little bowl of white
powder on the floor, and Gramp,
wearing a white apron and smoking,
said "look here m'boy," and held up
a big rat, beady-eyed, snake-tailed,
and I withered and crawled up into
myself and backed, on scratchy rodent's
feet, to the door, as Gramp, smiling and
smoking, swung the rat into a garbage
pail.

Words

Words that burn holes in cigarettes.
Words that stand like buildings
on street corners.
Sugary words on snow.
Words on the run like "tintinnabulation"
or on the rebound like "ding-dong"
or sitting on their asses like "plop" and "glop"
words to sing about like "serosanguineous"
words to write home about like "lachrymose"
tachycardic words to have a heart attack over,
sly words like "estimable"; soft words like "succor"
and "demur"; nonunion words like "whopper-doodle':
dirty words like "dipstick" and "fortissimo"; cute words
like "aver"; words that should not be said in public like
"medulla oblongata"; words for a rainy day like "lugubrious";
suspect words like "albeit"; Japanese words like "hitherto";
over-used words like "cool"; power words like "Ommm";
words no one wants to hear any more like "surreal"; words
that sound like loose change in your pocket like
"insufficient";
words and more words, up the ying-yang, down the hatch
as in the beginning, and forever.

Cooked

I was cook at Vagina Pizza in Cambridge, Massachusetts
and one night at end of shift a waitress asked
did I need a place to stay
and I said "no" and turned my back on her and walked out
carrying my suitcase and duffle bag—my ball and chain—
and slept in the bus station shelter until a cop woke me
and said "you can't sleep here," and I walked until dawn
while shiny police cruisers running smooth as vacuum cleaners
patrolled the empty streets.

Barefoot

Barefoot in the kitchen

and reading a book

as the radio plays

flutes and violins coming through

and a conductor, mane of hair waving

baton in swinging arm

and the emperor Hadrian

at Villa Adriana

and, hey, almost time for a snack

then a write

on yellow lined paper

as the breeze from the fan

tickles my legs

still muscular from walking

all these years

but now with red patches on my feet

from diabetes

or poor blood flow

(the doc doesn't know)

"sugar" from the matrilineal line

arterial heart disease from Pa

alcoholism from Grandma,

the frozen goggle-eyed shrew.

Thanks a lot, guys.

Prisoners

The bars
of this jail
are paper.
Dig a tunnel
but you
can't
get out.
There is
a warden
living
on every
block.
Rules
to obey:
they watch
you
come and
go
note how
you move
and what
you say.
They are

neighbors:

ones who

share

this torture

chamber.

Half-A-Cop

I was hitchhiking through Framingham,
Massachusetts, and a guy picked me up
and gave me a job
as security guard
at the Ford Auto plant
where I sat all night in a tiny shack
and checked trucks in and out
and on slow nights read a book
and put my feet up on the desk
and sometimes smoked pot.
My job was to step out and raise
a long aluminum pole to let trucks in.
One night I woke in an earthquake,
the shack trembling from the idle
of a twelve-wheeler loaded with
cars, and I stepped out, half-asleep
as I lifted the bar
the truck started through
and I lost my grip
and the pole fell over the cab
and bent in the shape of a horseshoe.
The truck driver had several kinds
of fits; some guy ran up to me and

screamed in my face, and the lights

in the yard came on bright as day.

I stayed awake the rest of that night

going out now and then

to lift the bent pole

just a little higher.

VIII

stuck with this

to live with this

don't have to agree

with this

but will die

with this and

no other

Struggle

I struggle out of bed

out of sleep

like wading ashore

to the bathroom

to piss

but no light no light

point it and listen

for the splash

but miss

now I am wide awake

damn it

and stalk the floor back to bed

a white square of light at my feet

and 3 A.M.

bewilderment

and

terror.

No Therapist

Sat on a park bench

in the sun

the cold wind

on my back

and read a newspaper

front to back

and not one fool

approached me

though

a few thought of it:

the worse ones

say "hello!"

and expect me

to respond in kind

and are pissed

when I don't

and mutter under

their breath

because their

expectations

have not been

met,

not knowing that

I do not exist to reinforce anyone's ego.

By-Pass

I need to go to the market
to buy unsalted bread
and unsweetened tea
and white meat not red;
don't want to have another
by-pass surgery
during which they ripped a vein out of my leg
chain-sawed my sternum
plugged the vein into a new outlet
and jump-started my heart.
Afterward, the doc came to my bed,
said "fine, you're fine," and
explained that the operation was "routine"
but I did not feel "fine" or "routine"
I felt as if dying
and had lost ambition to do anything
but lie in bed and
hope everyone left me alone
and no one asked "how do you feel?"
because I was sick of the question
sick of people asking
sick of hearing myself answer
and sick of myself too:

the suddenly fragile self
that had betrayed me
in so spectacular a fashion;
had left me hurt and stunned
like the apostles must have felt
when they saw Judas
with the soldiers.

The Park

1.
A jack hammer rippling
edges into my head;
tiny glinting leaves slip from
a tree in the squinting sun
and a black girl with blonde hair
says to her dog,
"are you fucking stupid
or what?"
She approaches my bench
asks for my empty coffee cup
for her dog, which I give
and the dog, name of Otis
chews as he lies in the shade.
The girl has a great rounded ass —
a double bubble —
but thick legs.
As she parades before me
her dog approaches and sniffs my
shoe.

2.
A crow came in on little

stanchion legs and
bounced once as it landed
and began to peck at some potato salad
spewed in the street—
and the yahoos became louder, to show their mothers
who failed them, that they exist
and a guy waiting for the bus
waited
and the stare-ers on benches stared at
all that isn't happening
and at all that never could
and I sat with my face to the sun
prepared to be rude
to anyone who came near.

3.

The park is nice
when no one there
is running his or her
mouth
but the blabbers are
everywhere,
unable to keep quiet
in love with the sound of their
voice,

logorrhea of the gums

they got,

blubberers,

polluting the air:

BAwah ba WAH bah wah wah

to the edge of the grave:

mine or theirs.

Spring

The budding trees have bloomed
like a girl out of puberty who
suddenly blossoms full-bodied
and lush. It'll never happen for
the girl again, but the trees do it
once each year, and each year it
is something to see and so, man,
is the girl.

The Long Walk

another MANPOWER job
where they send you out to work
and take half your pay
only it wasn't a bad job, this one:
mixing paints, putting
the cans into the arms
of a machine and
watching the machine jiggle like
a belly dancer...
I got off at four
and started to hitchhike
but could not get a ride
and all the drivers
looked smug, like bastards, laughing at me, and I thought
"fuck you assholes,
I will walk,"
and I started to walk
my back to the traffic
cars going past at
sixty, the bastards!
I was pissed: even if
a car stopped I would
not get in.

I marched like one of
Caesar's soldiers going
to meet the Gauls,
sweating out my ass;
it was hot, hazy, no
breeze, people moved
out of my way, I must not have looked normal.
I wasn't normal.
I was pissed.
I walked twelve miles
back to the place.
A girl who lived in
the apartment asked
how I got back and I
said "I walked."
She had a Mid-Eastern
look and was screwing
a black guy from Detroit who smoked pot and did
not talk.
Me, I wasn't screwing anyone
except myself.

Heartburn

The fan blows on my legs and beautiful feet
though red with splotches now
from diabetes
I was diagnosed with
at age 58
after I drove myself to the ER
with radiating chest pain
(heartburn, I'd told myself)
and was later operated on
due to arterial heart disease
and stayed in the dreadful hospital
for six days
waking at night to doom
in a cold sweat
and once, returning to bed from the bathroom,
over hearing my roommate say
to his visiting wife
"that guy is great;
he is quiet like me,"
and I felt a little ashamed
because
secretly, I had despised the guy.

Courtyard

I was alone in the courtyard

until some guy wearing red socks

and an Army cap turned backwards

sat and rolled a cigarette and

started to read a paperback;

then some pigeons flitted

from trees

and another guy walked through

reading text messages

and a girl on a bicycle

who looked like an Italian movie star

glided past

and a silver bird soared overhead

through blue sky

and another girl, with jugs that moved

like a waterbed,

pulled a dog past on a leash

and then everything returned to normal:

trees stood

sun shined

earth turned

and I was alone.

Attempted Murder, 3rd Degree

While driving to school one morning in my
'67 Chevy Nova I spotted Dicky,
who had all the answers in class,
walking
across the parking lot and
for laughs
I turned the car toward him
and he stopped,
his eyes growing bigger as I approached
but, the dumb bastard, refused to move
and I hit him
and he went onto the hood
then into the windshield and his feet went over
the roof
and in the rear view mirror I watched him drop
as if from out of the sky
and I thought "he's dead,"
but he looked up at me
as I bent over him
and the little prick stood
and limped into the school
and I was called to the vice-principal's office
and Mr. Connor, better known as Condor,

fixed his bird-of-prey eye on me
as he spoke of attempted murder
and said that Dicky's knee was screwed-up
and he could lose his Ivy League scholarship
because of it.
Being in the office was like being in a fishbowl
and I felt bad—not because of Dicky
(who could go to State College)
but because I was painfully hung over
and unable to respond intelligibly
to El Condor...
Later, a letter came to the house
from Dicky's lawyer
asking for thousands of dollars:
enough to pay an Ivy league tuition.

Heat

Six months in an icebox and
finally some heat:
the fan on top of the refrigerator
moves its head back and forth
like an electrified idiot;
I sit in shorts, no shirt
before the computer,
slight breeze through the window
and igloo people in the street
with their clothes off
white slug bodies burnt like lobsters;
plus beer drinkers, fried food eaters
slobs with guts like kegs;
and 16 year-olds pushing baby carriages
into futures of welfare
and low-paying jobs;
and homeless, in the park
drinking coffee brandy from
brown paper bags;
and a crackhead trying
to talk an ATM into more money;
also business people with their cheery
practiced hellos

and merchant souls…

The sun bakes the horizon brown

and the grass simmers on low:

Winter, the wicked witch

has melted like

the snow.

Punks

Standing on the main street of Framingham,
Massachusetts, holding my thumb up
in the air
and watching all the cars in the world
drive by me
and all the drivers look like assholes
to me
and a car goes past with some punks in it
and one of the punks gives me the finger
and I turn and chase the car
as the punks
point and laugh at me until
their car slows then stops at a red light
and I gain ground
and the smiles of the punks disappears
their eyes widen like dolls' eyes
and the car squeals out and I chase it
to the next light
and the punks in the back seat hop around
like monkeys in a cage
as I close the gap again
and the car shoots ahead
and I chase it to the next red light

which the car blows through

and I give up,

out of breath

still pissed

but not really

about

a bunch of punks.

IX

crows on a telephone line
cawing
an unlisted number

a noise outside the window—
the landlord walks
across the lot

going going gone
the fence flies over the ball—
it's a run home

The Irish Sea

The elevator goes up and down
as the ferry boat bobs
like a bar of soap
in a bathtub
and ocean waves rise to walls
and fall in avalanches —
smoke from my cigar is whipped away
like ghostly wraiths
to the stern
a football field away
from where I stand at the rail
of this steel toy vessel,
play thing of the sea,
and try to see into the future
which is all green-gray water
rising to a hillside
cascading to a plain
up-see-doosy and down again
it's no time for a swim
my knees go weak with the thought:
I sink like the Titanic into the briny salt
sea of myself.

Sunday

Sunday morning walking down O'Connell Street
in Dublin
a man beside me
his face red
pork pie hat on
he vomits into the gutter as
church-goers in their Sunday best,
ties and suits and gingham dresses,
all the shops closed
the Liffey River flows, but barely,
like a mud puddle, one that Joyce
made such a song and dance about—
dirty kids on the bridge say mister mister
give us pence!
Upheld hands like pigeons,
ragged clothes
I throw some crumbs
and they scramble, run—
a swan spreads its wings over the river
and I fly too
though feeling disreputable
in my jeans, lumberjack shirt
and with my hangover:

I walk back streets

and am followed by two mean-looking sons of Erin

I lose in an alley

sweating into my shirt until

I come back out onto O'Connell

and the wee freckle-faced red-haired folk

parade in their suits

on the Irish day of partial sanity.

x

a bus shudders to a stop —
I remember going Greyhound
across country

long wait in line
at the Post Office —
man mails a letter to China

the mean girl has
cannonballs
strapped to her chest

The Days of Our Lives

Grandma watches As the World Turns
as Gramp strolls through the living room;
his black garters hold up his black socks,
his t-shirt white, golfing hat on tilted;
he stops in the doorway, looks in, and says
"all that damn woman does is watch television,"
and turns away, jingling loose change in the
pocket of his Bermuda shorts. Gramp liked best
to be outside; had spent forty years cooped in-
side a bar; he took me, and my brother Mitch,
plus Uncle Albert, fly fishing on the Deerfield
River: Mitch cast and hooked a whopper — Uncle Albert
on the shoulder. Gramp walked into the stream,
hip-high wading boots on, fell and went under.
End of trip. Later, I went up the notch brook with
my rod and reeled in a rainbow trout that Grandma
cleaned and cooked; Uncle Albert, seated at the
dinner table, stared like he hated my guts, which
he did: mine and his own, he was resentful, bitter,
too late for things his sister and brother got, like
attention; he was the rotten baby of his family, his
talents, like himself, ignored; his face become sepulchral.

The Drunkards

My Aunt Louise the beautiful, sexy
was asked to pose for PLAYBOY and
said no; she was brassy, wore fire
engine red lipstick and drank the men
under the table, like her mother, the
alky, Grandma Murphy, oddly frozen
in her chair and smile that never showed
teeth, she died in the nut house of
"tuberculosis." I was a teenager then and
one of her pallbearers. At the wake a guy
asked me who I was and I said "pallbearer"
and at the funeral the guy called me "Paul."
After the service everyone went to my Uncle's
house and got loaded, including me and my
cousin who got into a fight and smashed the
furniture in his bedroom and my Uncle, his
face stern, arrived in the doorway and put his
arm around mine and my cousin's shoulders
and gave us "the talk"—how he, Uncle, and my
dead father had been buddies—and I was the
"spitting image" of my Dad—and all the good
times the two had had, but how they never
crossed a certain line of decency...The arm on

my shoulders, over the years, got heavier each time applied, but "the talk" never changed.

As the Worm Turns

I am 58 years old, four
years younger than Gramp
when he cashed in the chips
while lying in bed, a "hospital"
bed that was elevated by a
crank at the foot, because he
had apnea along with cancer,
high BP, asthma, a bunch of
stuff, lucky he was to make it
long as he did; he tried out a
red convertible the year he
died, drove us kids, me, my
brother, two Baguette brothers
to the beach and while there
Gramp ripped a fart and Donny
Baguette laughed like it was the
funniest thing he'd ever heard.
I pulled a sucker fish from the
river that day; it bit and I felt the
tug and weight of the thing and I
heave-hoed the pole and the fish
come flying out of the water like
it had decided to jump out the

river. Gramp buried the sucker
in the garden to fertilize flowers
Grandma had planted. The Baguette's
were going to the state park one
day and said I could come too and
I ran home to get my suit and towel
but when I got back they were gone.
Mr. Baguette was odd because he
would not look at anyone or answer
when spoken to, and Mrs. Baguette
walked around in her underwear;
Donny later became an RN like his
mom but the youngest sister went
to the nut house, and Charlie Baguette,
who was my age, and nut house material
too, became a computer programmer.
Gramp bought steel poles and had them
tied to the backyard fence — for the
basketball court he was going to have
built in the driveway — but the poles
never moved off the fence; they hung
for years and rusted, and anytime I
wanted to play basketball I had to go
to the Garibaldi's across the street and
used their court in the corner of their

backyard: in my senior year of high
school I made the team but did not
play much and lost confidence so that
by the end of the season I did not want
to play anymore and I blamed it all on
Gramp because of those stupid poles
he never put up
like he said he would.

About the Author:

Wayne F. Burke was born in Adams, Massachusetts and raised by his paternal grandparents. As a boy he was an All-Star baseball player, and in High School an All Class-A football player. He attended the University of Massachusetts—where he was a member of the freshman football team—and three other institutions of higher learning before graduating from Goddard College in 1979. His work history includes stints as bartender, moving man, cook, machine shop operator, sign painter, substitute school teacher, carpenter, truck driver, book reviewer (for the Burlington Free Press newspaper, Burlington, Vermont), and, for the past four years, LPN in a nursing home. His stories, essays, reviews, and poems have appeared in numerous publications. *Words that Burn* is his first published poetry collection.

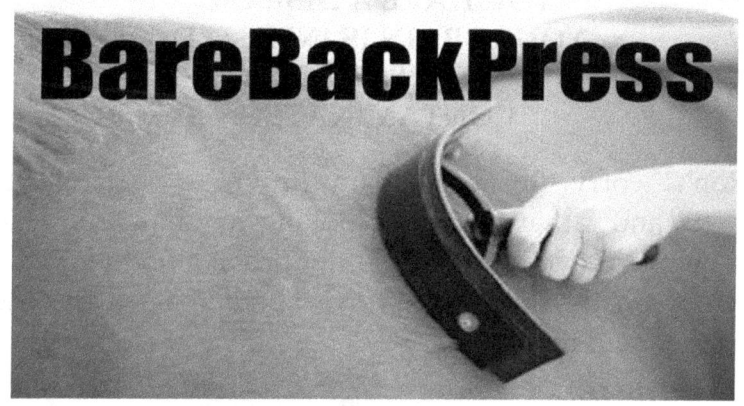

Also from
BareBackPress

The Cure for Consciousness
Peter Jelen

YOU HAVE A DISEASE.
YOUR BRAIN IS INFECTED.
POISONED.
CONTAMINATED.

But don't worry. Ernie Lobe, a fifty-four year old baker, sociopath, and father of two is looking for the cure, which he thinks he may have found. The only problem is there's a slight side-effect...death. But don't worry about that either, because you can get paid to die.

$12.99
132 Pages
6" x 9"
ISBN -13: 978-0988075061
BISAC: Fiction/ General

Unwrapped:
The BareBack Anthology

Unwrapped: The BareBack Anthology is a collection of innovative poetry from poets speckled around the world who have been featured in BareBack Magazine, an online publication dedicated to BareBack writers. People who aren't afraid to take off their gloves and give the world sincere, unpretentious, honest writing that has punch.

$17.99
136 Pages
6" x 9"
ISBN 13: 978-0988075047
BISAC: Poetry/General

Old Gods for New
Mike Algera

At a sidewalk sale
you will meet a dealer
he will tell you
he has monuments of old gods
for sale, "Pick a God,
and worship however you please." ~ Excerpt from Old Gods for New

Old Gods for New reflects upon personal triumphs and demons, love and longing, the past and never-was; musings that spark both the artistry of playful banter as well as lyrical madness. Writing that is quirky yet daring, combining scratch words into something new.

$19.99
138 Pages
6" x 9"
ISBN-13: 978-0988075078
BISAC: Poetry/ General

Little Human Accidents:
Damon Ferrell Marbut

Damon Ferrell Marbut devastates the notion of apology in poetry with a tender recklessness in *Little Human Accidents*, poems that examine a personal evolution of sexuality and identity while treating the unavoidable step towards adulthood like a punching bag, especially in his free flowing self reflexive poems like *Mornings Like This* and *So What*.

$19.99
150 pages
6" x 9"
ISBN 13: 978-0988075092
BISAC: Poetry/ General

The Big Picture
Andrew J. Simpson

I WALKED UP BEHIND GOD AND STUCK A SIGN ON HIS BACK. IT SAID "FREE WILL," OR "KICK ME."

The government is taxing your dreams and moments are being captured and held against their will. Murphy's Law is suspended pending the outcome of a constitutional challenge; a best-selling author writes and publishes the same novel fifteen times without anyone catching on, and all of humanity is put into receivership over a missing cup of coffee.

Andrew J. Simpson's debut anthology is a highly creative journey through the world of the surreally real. Savour the fantastical and the mundane, every nuance and notion that makes up The Big Picture.

www.barebackpress.com

www.ingramcontent.com/pod-product-compliance
Lightning Source LLC
Chambersburg PA
CBHW060328050426
42449CB00011B/2696